AF364654

ISBN: 978-84-09-59125-1

Montenegro
A Reverie of Whispers

Franca Sol

Illustrated by Branka Kovačević

Budva
Story of Two Yachts

Two yachts are docked
In front of the majestic walls of Budva's Old Town
Dancing on sea waves, side by side.
One gleams pitch black,
The other pure pearl.
THE JETSETTER is boldly emblazoned on the dark hull,
Felicità elegantly etched on the off-white.

The yin and the yang in the parking stand.
I choose *felicità*.

But you don't have a boat... they say.
But I have a life.

Bečići
A Palačinke Fascination

Montenegro has a lover
Over which it is obsessed.
The country's fascination: palačinke
Is the first word a foreigner learns.

Layer after layer,
Bite after bite,
Montenegrin palačinke cheers up the day
Of the picker and the gourmet.

Palačinke it is,
In every city, on every street,
On the corner of any hood.
Smell, taste, indulge!

Slowly or voraciously
The point is to delight.
Bites of happiness
For every palate.

Find it at the corner café of Kotor Old Town,
At the street food stands of Bečići Bay,
At the poshest outlets of Tivat frontline.
The smell of palačinke is a centrifuge force
Among the old and the child,
The local and the visitor,
The wealthy, the skint,
The cheat dieter, the bon vivant,
The coastal lover and the orophile.

Thin layers of pleasure and chocolate sin,
A bicolored formation
Becomes an edible recreation
Of Crna Gora, the sea-embraced black hill.

Is that what makes palačinke so distinct?
Its resemblance to this land
Of mountains and gorges, of pebbles and sea?
Folly!

It is but a reflection of the appetite
Of a Montenegrin gourmand.

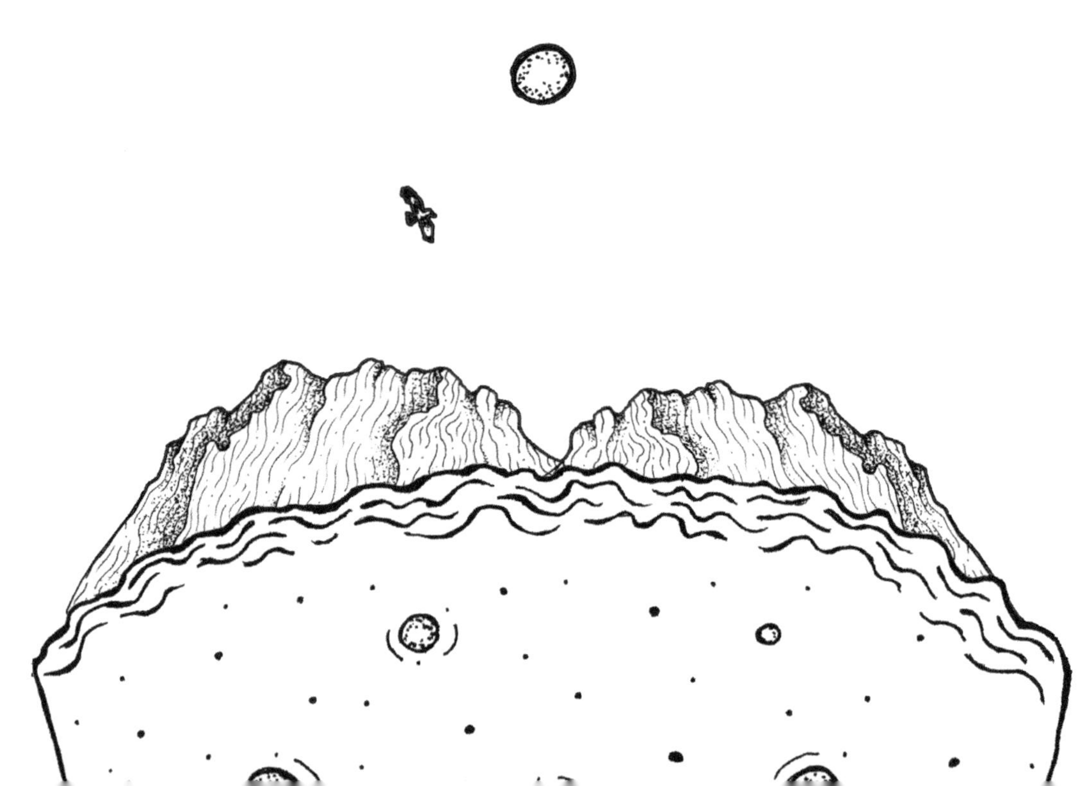

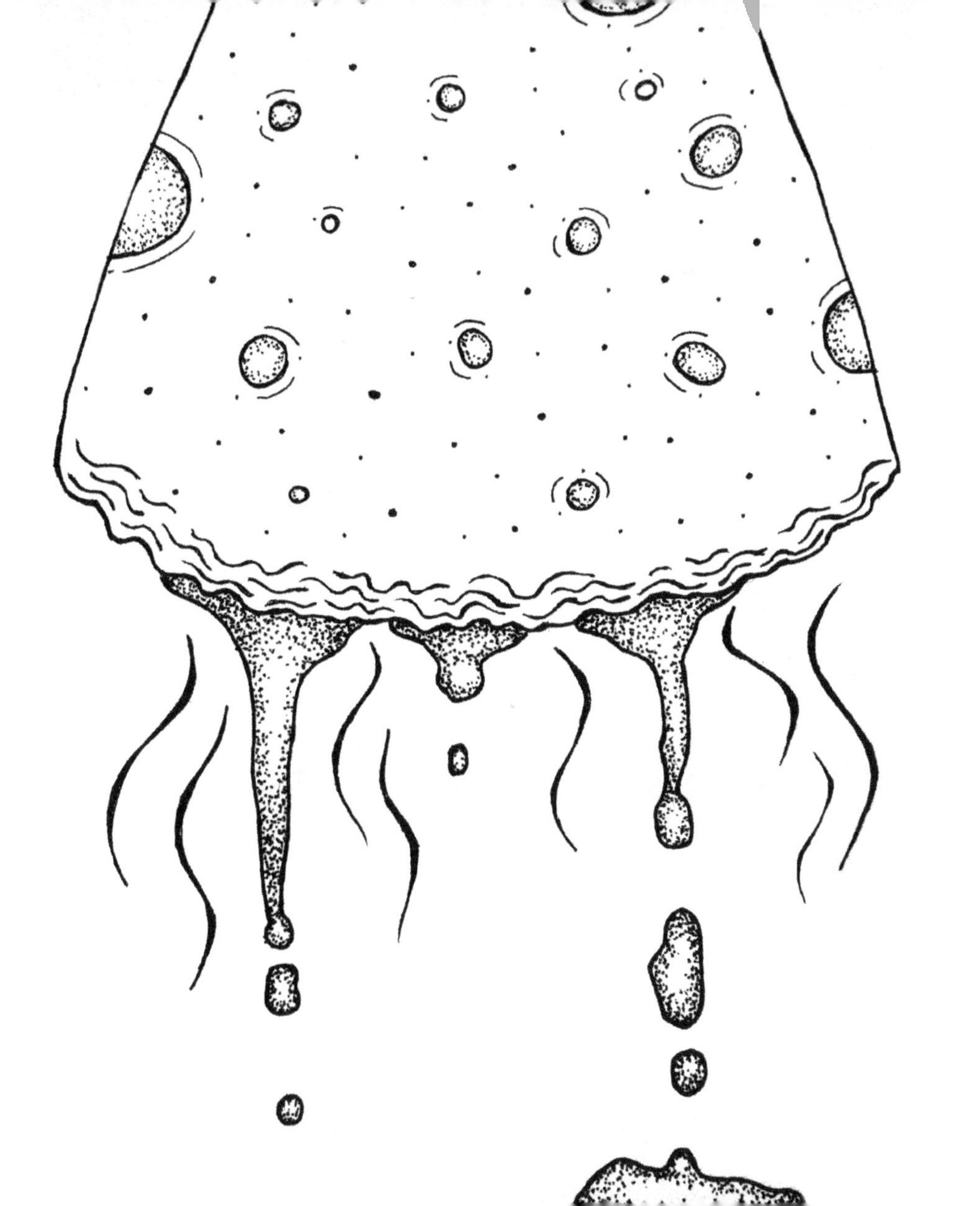

Rafailovići
Morning in the Promenade

Pink lipstick and a blue apron,
Morning time on the promenade.
Rafailovići awakens
To the sweeps of her broom.

Brush after brush,
Like the waves of the sea,
She readies the café
For the regulars to come in.

A straw hat and a cigar
Enters and sits at the left-hand table.
He is the old painter of the village
Who once loved and still does.

Metal glasses pretend to read the newspaper
While his memory travels back to the old days
When he painted his wife and muse
At the beach with the hollow rocks.

Firm steps, a new customer strolls in,
The smell of the fish trailing him.
His order, ready before he gets close!
A strong espresso, a sip of repair
After a night far from shore's care.

His metal wheelbarrow outside
Full to the top with the catch of the day,
Freshly captured seabass and dorada
Ready to be delivered to the restaurant next door.

The old Maltese, half-blind, half-lame,
Barks non-stop, a loyal claim.
The fisherman feeds the cats outdoors,
But to pet his friend, he forgets.

Now it's the turn of the chatty cashier,
Who works at the supermarket down the road.
Her husband just dropped her,
Kiss to cheek, grumpy-faced, but wanting more.

A cappuccino with two sugars
And a slice of honey cake
To match her manicure's hue,
Ahead of the busy day.

And with her pink lips and her blue apron,
She is the one who every day,
Every season, sun or rain,
Sweetens our morning in the promenade of
Rafailovići.

Coffee after coffee,
Smile after smile,
She serves her old customers
and those like me, new to town.

OPEN

Bar
You are

Antibari — 'on the other side.'
Your walls perpetually compared
To the city across the waves.
A Roman curse to shed,
Likeness to forget.
Majesty shines,
Walls stand high,
You are,
Bar.

This nonet draws inspiration from the Roman name 'Anti-bari,' a reference to the ancient city of Bar in present-day Montenegro. The prefix "anti-" suggests "opposite" or "across from," possibly distinguishing it from Bari, the city across the Adriatic Sea in what is now Italy.

Ulcinj
You, Me, the Sea

You.
You and me.
Together: The sea.
A wave arises.
It is a little one. We jump!
A bigger wave comes next, it is gone.
Again the calm, until the next.
Dots of water on the horizon emerge.
And come and go.
But we are still here,
We are sea.
We.

Skadar
Wild Horses

Warm wind caresses my forehead,
Eyes wide open to the horizon.
My gallop surges with full power,
Unfettered and untamed.

Beneath the open sky, I roam.
A spirit unbound, on my own.
Amongst ancient trees and stones,
I race the wind, vivid and wild.

I am free, indomitable,
Untied from everything.
I melt into the vastness
Of rocky mountains and bushy fields.

But Skadar, you are a harness,
a magnetic field.
I rest at the feet of your shore,
Your tranquil surface a repose.

I feel you, I sense you,
Connected to everything.
The deepness of your waters,
A sweet calling from within.

And I come,
For my freedom is foolish without your anchor.
You ground me, allowing me to be,
And I choose: Surrender.

Prokletije
The Forest Fairy

Hidden by a pointed, hooded cape,
Like lightning under the rain,
A shadow descends
The mountain summit of Prokletije.

Who is this shadow
Fusing with earth, water and wind?
A blend of lightness and strength
That takes my breath and runs away.

The shepherd's dog,
My companion on the trek,
Chases the shadow and joins the jog.
Two souls dancing a gallop.

Was it so foggy that I couldn't spot him before?
No, it was not.
So who is it
Under that hood?

Soon he is gone.
Wind, water,
And the smell of the earth
Are all that are left.

What are you? Where did you go?
I can't explain.
So I continue down the trail
… but you took my breath away.

The generous millennial forest
Offers me its cover
To pause and breathe
Sheltered from the daunting rain.

Hi!
I turn to see you, nested under the trees,
Panting, recovering from the run
With hands on knees.

Hello!
And I turn away
Pretending not to feel
His magnetic power.

Do you believe in the wisdom of nature? his voice echoes.
I do.
Then ask permission to step in
And come with me to the depths of the forest.

The hood pushed back,
Green eyes revealed.
I follow and join his walk
Two hearts beating a gallop.

Hug the tree, ask its advice
Of anything and it will tell.
Alas! The tree might say
… but you took my heart away.

Who are you? How did you learn
All that nature wants to tell?
Earth, fire, water, and air
Are those of which you are made?

The torn sky deepens its cry,
Darkness and fog blinding my sight.
Take my hood, give me your hand.
One soul melted at a gallop.

Is it that dim that I can't see one step in front
of me?
Yes, it is.
But he is the one
Now guiding me.

And soon we arrive,
Back to the plains.
The clouds are gone,
A break from rain.

Who are you, who from nowhere
Appeared under the rain
At the top of Prokletije?

To nowhere you disappeared
As soon as the storm went
On the plains of Prokletije.

... and you took my soul away.

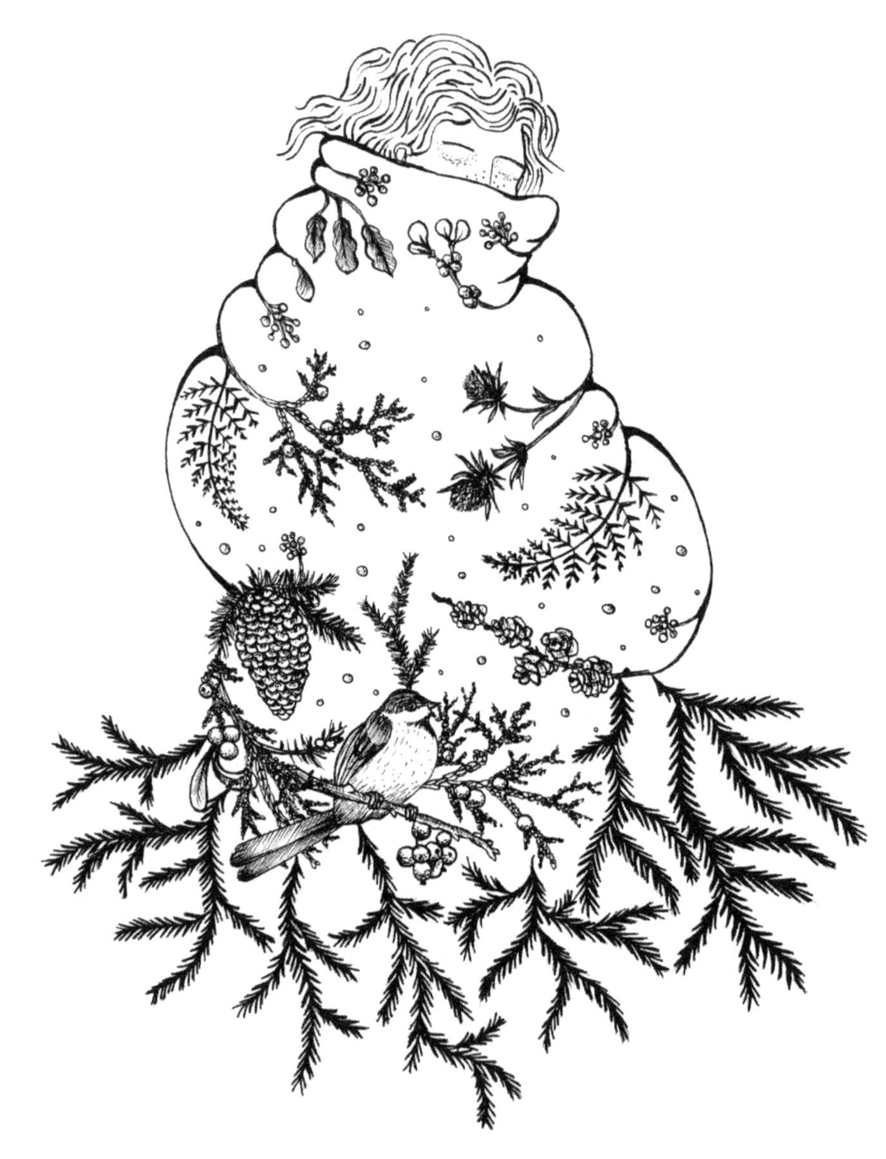

Kolašin
A Haiku of Blueberries and Blues

The snowflakes fall
Burying blueberry bushes.
Kolašin winter.

How deep to bury
Your blues, sorrows, and fears
In the snow of Kolašin?

The thin bark succumbs
Choked by the grip of the frost.
Flakes of frozen tears.

Two seasons have passed.
Snow melted by the sun,
The blueberries bloom.

How deep did you think
You could bury your blues,
Sorrows and fears?

Shades of violet,
Obliterated blindness
In purple blossoms.

Not a choke, but an embrace.
Not a grip to drag you down
But to hold you tight.

Denial melted.
The embrace of the deep winter.
A fearless breath.

Handpicked blueberries
One, and two, and a thousand more
Until a naked bush. Rebirth.

Biogradska Gora
A Family Feud

This is the story
Of Biogradska Lake. A circle
With no beginning and no end.

Home to two families, once related by blood,
Living in facing houses,
The sole inns at the park's slopes.

Me, you. A line.
These are my tourists,
Lodging in my house.

Those are yours.
Stay away from my business,
a big warning sign.

Are you staying there?
Ugh, I don't recommend.
Food is terrible, so is the stay.

Over there have you booked?
The coffee is awful,
You will wake up in a bad mood.

Once kin, you are now my enemy
Since we argued once
Over the price of the tourists sleeping on our land.

And I will fight you, my shotgun at hand
To defend my business.
Do not cross the line.

Dobro jutro, welcome to my guesthouse.
It's such a cute place,
with its shiny yellow tiles.

Dobar dan, feel at home my lovely guests!
With our blue window shutters
Our cottages offer deep rest.

Blue window shutters, shiny yellow tiles,
Watching each other
With resentful eyes.

Me, you. A line.
These are my tourists
Lodged at my house.

Shiny yellow tiles, blue window shutters,
Melt into a green dot
When viewed from the mountain's top.

Not you, not me,
Not a line
But the circled lake of Biogradska.

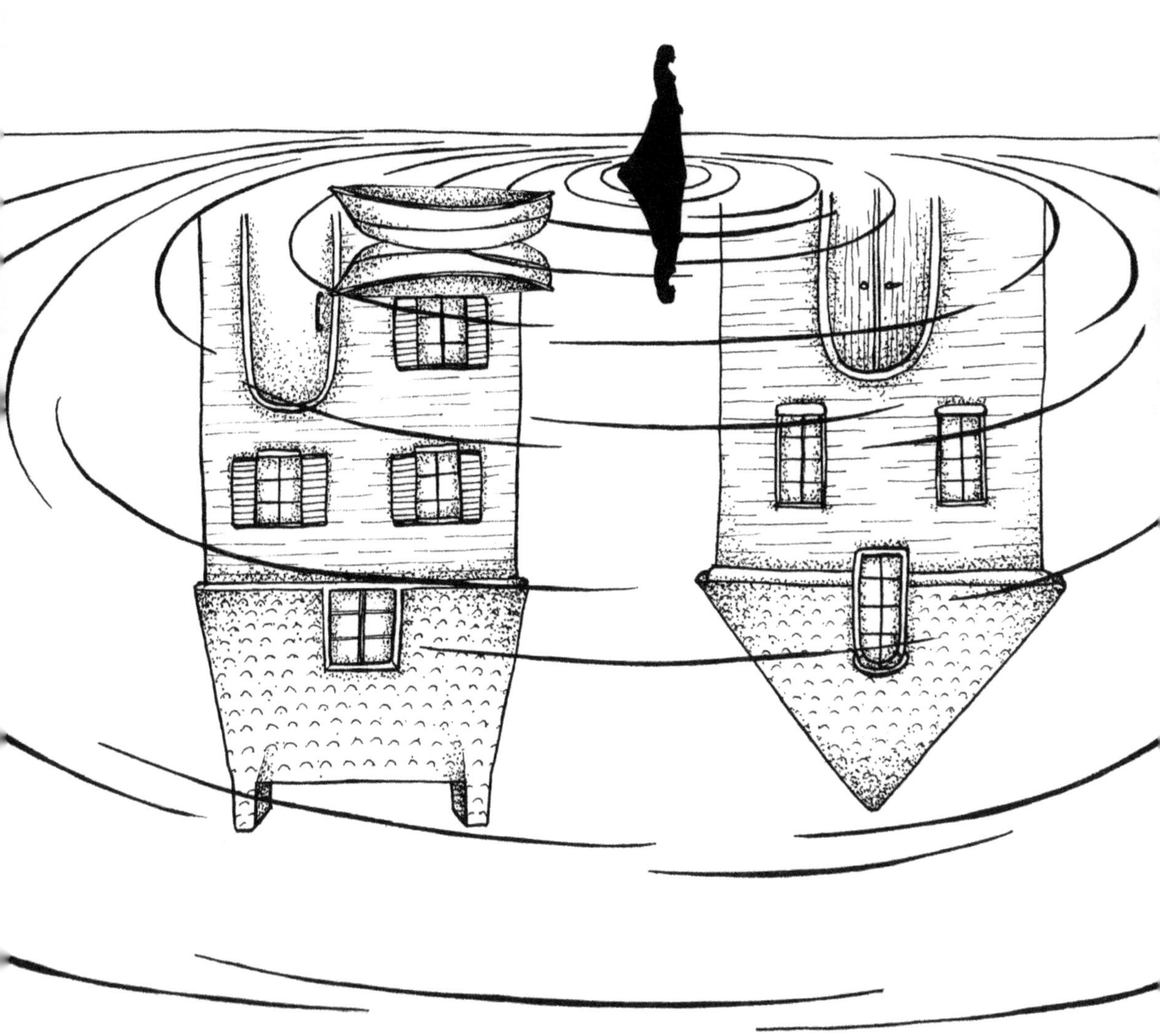

Cetinje
The Heart

Montenegro has a heart that gives away all its radiance.

Where is it? In the old capital of Cetinje?

Hidden behind the monastery walls of Saint Peter?

Or under the red paint of King Nicola?

Perhaps beneath the tiles of Njegošva streets?

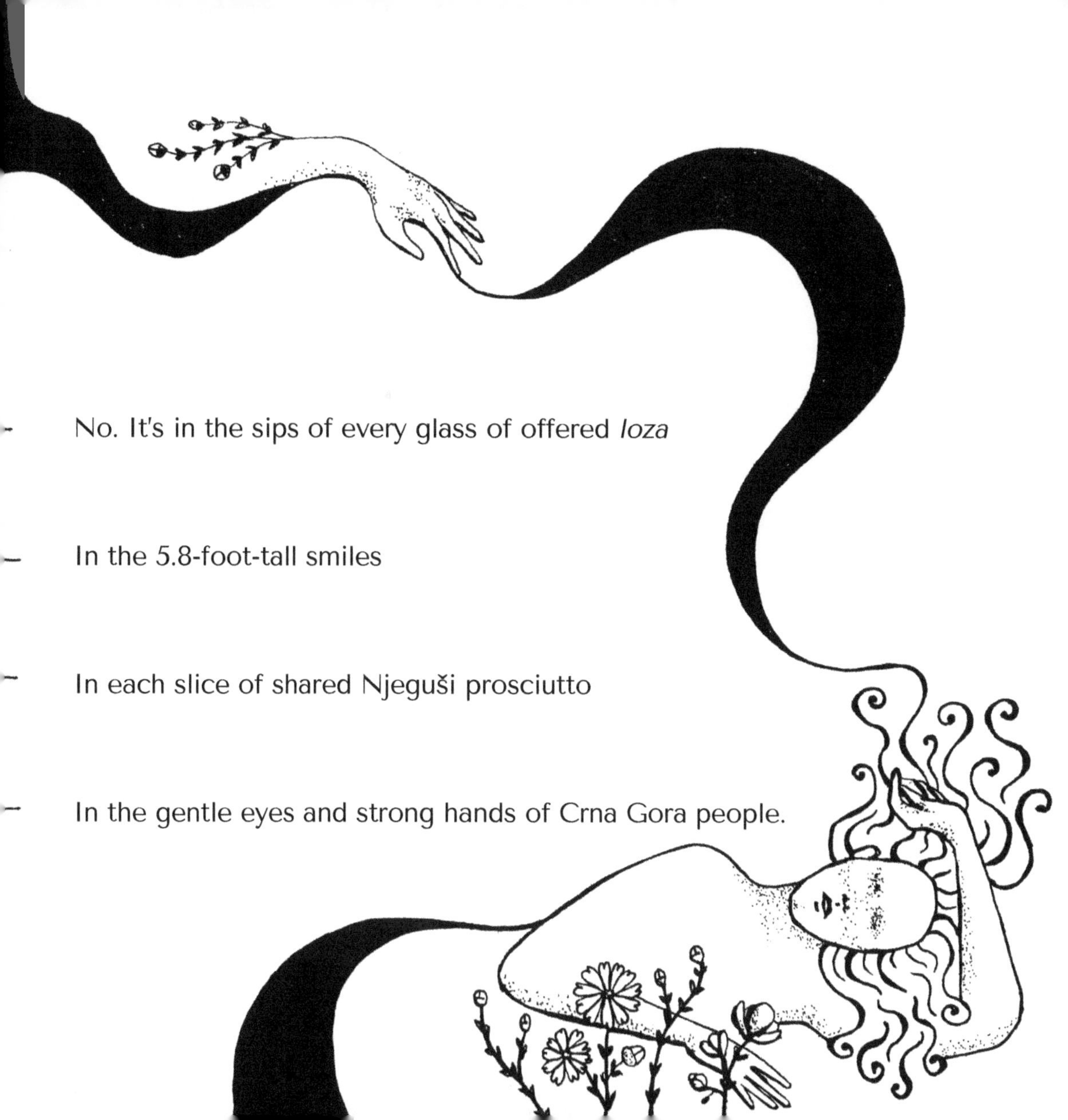

No. It's in the sips of every glass of offered *loza*

In the 5.8-foot-tall smiles

In each slice of shared Njeguši prosciutto

In the gentle eyes and strong hands of Crna Gora people.

Kotor
An Ode to Pirates and Mermaids

Dusk time has come
To the inner walls of old Kotor.
This is the time to hear the whines
Of the crippled pirate ghost.
Uneven cobblestones, cold mediaeval façades
Become silent and listen to the grumbles
Of that ill-tempered captain
Vessel long-ago sunken.

Broken by the iron chains of Kotor's defence! he rages
My ship I lost, my life as well.
What an irony it is, the wrecks of such a magnificent boat
Built for bounties and golden coins,
Now filled with plastic and waste
Left by visitors to Kotor Bay.

Treasures and pearls, fine wines, and textiles
Replaced by pollution of all types.

Dawn time has come
To butterfly-shaped Kotor Bay.
This is the time to hear the cry
Of the once beloved Crna Gora mermaid.
Dolphins and waves
Slow their ride
Saddened by her sobs,
The heart-broken Siren of Old Kotor.

What an irony it is! My melodious voice
For sailors to tease, merchants to please
Ceased to echo in this bay.
Deafened now by the self-welcoming scream
Of each cruise shouting: hi!
In the blink of an eye, yelling: bye!
The days have ceased when I sang, whispered, and en-
chanted
Vessels and boats to my whims.

Cruise after cruise, invading the bay.
To war! Shouts the pirate,

Get out! cries the mermaid.
But their voices are silenced,
No one hears them,
The cruisers are in a rush
Hurry! No time to lose!
Visit and leave for the next port.

Only cold walls and uneven cobblestones,
Saddened dolphins and angry waves,
Listen to the voices of the crippled pirate
and the heartbroken mermaid
Who between sobs and laments,
Bottles of plastic, fumes, and waste,
Bravely try to save
Kotor Bay.

Perast
Promises like Skin

Promises that you made to protect with your walls,
like a skin from the outer world.

Ephemeral though is the touch of the salty sea, a caress.

Remembrance of time in stand still, noble embrace of
your people and your land,

And of me, the newcomer sheltered in your arms.

Skin, a fine line shielding the in, enveloping the out,

Teetering in the temptation of change, a truce,
a breath in time's ethereal dance.

Franca Sol

is a captivating literary voice who weaves tales that transcend borders and capture the essence of diverse landscapes. Expressing genuine love for the countries in which she resides through art and literature, she brings readers on enchanting journeys of cultural and self discoveries.

Follow her work at francasolauthor.wordpress.com and on Instagram @montenegroreverie / @littleyemen.

Branka Kovačević

is a versatile illustrator known for her imaginative approach to storytelling through art. With a knack for adapting her style to the essence of the literature, she creates detailed drawings and paintings that inhabit a sweet spot between the tangible and the fantastical. Kovačević's work draws people into stories with relatable yet dreamlike visuals.

See her work at behance.net/banjakovacd0fd

Felicia Campbell

is a writer and editor who specialises in collaborations with non-native English speakers. She loves helping to bring diverse stories to life, while maintaining each author's unique voice.

Find her @hungryfi on Instagram and at feliciacampbell.com.